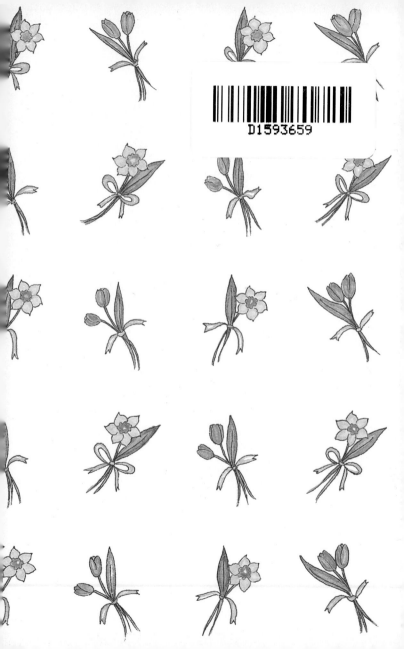

Dedicated
to my dad

To:

From:

# HOPE
# IS REAL

Written and Illustrated
by
Susan Squellati Florence

The C.R. Gibson Company, Norwalk, Ct. 06856

Hope is seen
      in the eyes...

Hope is heard
      in the voice...

Hope is held
      in the heart.

Hope is alive...
it is all around us.

Susan
Florence

Hope is the oak tree within the acorn.

Hope is the winged butterfly

within the cocoon.

Hope is the first rosebud
        of Spring,
        awakening in the stem
        of Winter's rose.

Hope is not blind.
Hope sees beyond
to what is.

lope sees
through the clouds
to the mountain tops,
and journeys
over the high peaks,
Knowing that on the
other side
a green valley awaits.

Hope is invisible ...

yet it can be seen
when the eyes
are closed.

Hope sees the real light
of the sun
as it shines within ...

and the real power
of love
as it fills the heart.

Hope sees
beyond our differences
to oneness...

and beyond
our appearances
to the heart.

Hope knows...
goodness lives
everywhere
in this world,

and miracles
are happening
everyday.

Hope lives
    with acceptance...
    of the unknowing
    every day.

Hope does not ask
when the darkness
will end...

Hope wonders
when the light
will begin.

Hope is...
a way of seeing,
a way of believing,
a way of knowing.

Hope is alive,
Hope is here,
Hope is real.

Have hope.
Be hope.
Live hope.
Love hope.

HOPE.

By Susan Squellati Florence

Friendship Is A Special Place
Babies Take Us On A Special Journey
A Book Of Loving Thoughts
A Gift Of Time
Your Journey
With Friends
The Heart Of Christmas
Hope Is Real